A Haiku For You

By

David G. Barbour

A Haiku For You

By

David G. Barbour

authorHOUSE®

AuthorHouse™
1663 Liberty Drive
Bloomington, IN 47403
www.authorhouse.com
Phone: 1-800-839-8640

First published by AuthorHouse   07/25/2011

ISBN: 978-1-4634-1341-5 (sc)
ISBN: 978-1-4634-1340-8 (hc)
ISBN: 978-1-4634-1757-4 (ebk)

Library of Congress Control Number: 2011908863

Printed in the United States of America

Catch one drug dealer
Soon another will take his place
Crime's vicious cycle

First date question asked
How do you make your living?
No job defines me

Compliments given
Even more gifts have I sent
Yet she is not mine

Raindrops sheeting down
Cars speed by without headlights
No way to see them

The bluest of eyes
Everything a guy could want
Oh, to be her man

All you knew of life
Crimes, drugs, abject poverty
The world says sorry

Question everything
Then wait for the depression
Ignorance is bliss

Black eyes and bruises
Given to her by the man
Who claims he loves her

Silence, cat caller
Let her walk unmolested
She does not want you

Amazing diet
Eat less food than you burn off
Then you will lose weight

Ovaries and breasts
Neither one measures women's worth
Gauge her mind instead

Comic book heroes
How I long for your powers
To make me special

Bed of rose petals
My hands are your eyes' blindfold
My mouth says don't peek

Could be my soulmate
Too bad I think you're ugly
Love is never blind

So pretty you are
At least when I am lonely
And have been drinking

Five and six year olds
Cursing more than most adults
Angels they are not

Four children you claim
All by different mothers
Dude, use a condom

A dozen flowers
With which to ask forgiveness
For my one time fling

Soldiers sent to die
By leaders who think terror
Has a real army

Soaking in bubbles
I close my eyes and think of
The day I met you

Rush hour train car
People on top of people
Reminds me of sheep

Ignored by your love
Taken for granted daily
You deserve better

Driver needs license
Contractor needs a permit
Parent needs nothing

Married for ten years
My wife is now a stranger
Whom I can't talk to

My myth makes more sense
No way, my myth makes more sense
Religious debate

Paycheck to payback
No way for humans to live
Money is evil

Boxes stare at me
Filling me with utter dread
Moving is the worst

Athletes must pretend
They are modest just to be
Liked by foolish fans

Wears the tightest clothes
In her mind, she's so sexy
Key words: in her mind

One man for money
One for sex, one for convo
How women should date

The gorgeous girl who
Say nothing valuable is
A waste of beauty

My promise to you
Affection that knows no bounds
Love that just won't quit

Real woman feels fat
Skinny actress told to eat
Neither one can win

It should have been me
The one you pledged yourself to
On your wedding day

Fifty-three countries
But treated like only one
Such is Africa

Your words say one thing
Your actions say another
Which should I believe?

Our love is still young
So your quirks still amuse me
Soon they'll annoy me

Old men make the laws
Telling women what to do
With their own bodies

If you had said yes
All of me would have been yours
No was what you said

Headphones on your ears
Music so loud people stare
You shut out the world

The same, tiresome tale
Straight girls get drunk and make out
Bisexual chic

Just this once she said
No one ever has to know
Spouses included

Clothes go round and round
Hypnotizing to the eye
I can't look away

Unruly children
Acting out for attention
They don't get at home

Flirting with a girl
I say the wrong thing and she
Smiles and walks away

Go on with your life
Pretending it all matters
When it might not, chief

You left me today
and wouldn't tell me why. Was that
too much to ask?

Poor whites and poor blacks
Have more in common than they
Would care to admit

A lump on the breast
She suspects but won't admit
It might be cancer

Here I go again
Spending money I don't have
On stuff I don't need

Ladies' man is praised
Woman dates men in the same way
We call her a slut

An hour has passed
My watch tells me the cold truth
I have been stood up

No time left for me
Work is all you care about
I thought I meant more

A pleasant surprise
You said I love you without
Me saying it first

No compliment tops
What you tell me every day
By being my girl

We cast shame on those
who love differently from
ourselves. Shame on us.

Even at your worst
When your hair looks a hot mess
You are still gorgeous

Frozen stiff I was
Until you smiled and touched me
Then warmth coursed through me

Broken promises
By now I should know better
Than to believe you

Trapped inside my mind
A darker place you've not known
Help me to escape

Wife wears a sweatshirt
Husband wears shorts and sandals
Which season is it?

He buys her a drink
Thinking that entitles him
To conversation

Your pillow smelled like
apples. Now that you've left me,
it smells like nothing.

Welcome to a world
Of festered vacuity
A socialite's life

Stop, don't say a word
You will just ruin the mood
I already know

Drugs don't control me
I can quit at any time
Lies of an addict

Fans cheer one minute
Boo the same player the next
So much for fealty

If I don't see it
Maybe it doesn't exist
Ostrich in the sand

A pitiful sight
To see people taking pride
In their ignorance

To be immortal
Would mean nothing without you
By my side always

To replace her sons
The mother buys a new puppy
Empty nest syndrome

Babe, do I look fat?
My wife asks me this knowing
There's no good answer

The girl of my dreams
Lives a thousand miles away
Long distance heartbreak

My guardian angel
You're never there to save me
From disappointment

A perfect friendship
Until the day we had sex
Now it is ruined

Easy to complain
Much harder to be happy
Which road will you choose?

These drugs I ingest
Make me feel like a genius
Even though I'm not

A dead dog causes
tears to fall but a dead man
means nothing to her

Today it's maybe
Yesterday was I don't know
Indecisive girls

One drunk uncle
Two aunts who had abortions
Family scandals

Young couple kissing
Hands all over each other
Get a room, you two

Hands out for candy
Children go trick or treating
With parents in tow

Picking on the weak
The bully always assures
Himself of winning

A mistake was made
It happened the day I said
I stopped loving you

We fight all the time
But there is no one else I
Would rather fight with

Rushed to get married
Thought her life would be complete
Now she is divorced

My child the stranger
Used to tell me everything
He keeps secrets now

I fell hard for you
It is just too bad you were
Not there to catch me

Your heart is broken.
Don't worry, I will fix it
with my special glue.

Can't stay in one spot
Must keep lying and moving
Fugitive women

The saddest thing
When a bride's wedding day is
Her happiest day

Pure coincidence
Us chancing to meet like that
On a jet airplane

Old guy creeps me out
Undressing me with his eyes
Says a teenage girl

First black president
So racism must be dead
Au contraire, mon frére

Tears I shed for you
I wish I could uncry them
Since you aren't worth them

My wounds have not healed
Although time was my doctor
He could do nothing

You watched me while I
slumbered and I have never
felt more weirded out

As the crazed man raves
People give him wide berth lest
His crazy rubs off

Let's travel in space
So we can stay young and in
love outside of time

Anger consumes me
Without an outlet I fear
It will destroy me

Her moods burn too bright
Too manic and too depressed
My bipolar friend

The insecure bride
Makes her bridesmaids look ugly
So she looks better

We're treading water
No longer in love but not
Out of love either

Dumb questions are asked
By reporters to coaches
In press conferences

My cry for help comes
late at night and no one is
awake to hear it

Standing ovations
Meant for live shows and not for
Movie theatres

I go to my left
He steps to his right starting
Our own sidewalk dance

In a crowded park
A man sits bleeding and no
one stops to help him

All generations
think they will see the world end.
Earth ignores them all

No name for parents
who lose children; if there were,
it would not hurt less

Jaded psych nurses
Treat their patients like garbage
Just for being sick

Misbehaving babe
Gets smiles from adults when she
Needs reprimanding

Slain black man ignored
Pretty white girl is murdered
Everyone cares then

Bundled up in bed
There is nothing I crave more
Than your warm embrace

As the days float by
It becomes more apparent
No girl will love me

Joyous reunions
Hugs and kisses all around
At every airport

Her simplest statement
Leads me to overthinking
And into a funk

Thanksgiving dinner
After the turkey is gone
Drowsiness ensues

Hotter than Hades
The heat is a blanket that
Wraps me too tightly

Thoughts race through my mind
How I long to turn them off
So I can have peace

No matter my words
I do care if I am liked
And I always will

All of me is now
wrapped up in all of you; we
two have become one

Every Christian loves
the Lord unless it's raining.
His bed is God then

Doctors only guess
At what is wrong with you and
Sometimes they are wrong

A young girl in love
So caught up in her feelings
She can lose her way

The more words she spoke
The more I wondered what I
Ever saw in her

Woman I can have
I don't want; I desire the
Unattainable

Pants below the waist
With your underwear showing
You look like a fool

A bible buffet
Dine on the scriptures you like
Leave the rest behind

Uniforms or not
Disobedient students
Will still misbehave

Courtly love's rubric
Pretty words that mean nothing
And cheapen romance

Human vanity
Having children just to say
Look, another me

Oh God, hear my thoughts
But only the nicest ones
Otherwise, butt out

Everyone has eyes
But none has two that are quite
As captivating

Synonym for saint
A politician is not
Don't judge him like one

Love or ownership?
Which describes my feelings? I
fear it's the latter

Parents' worst mistake
Thinking toddlers will behave
In a restaurant

No matter the laws
Women who want abortions
Will get abortions

The human body
Keeps time better than any
Clock ever devised

A waste of ad space
Telling people not to smoke
By speaking of health

My quest has ended
Since I have found love with you
I need look no more

Trend of the moment
Saving the environment
How long will it last?

Too much to handle
Can't deal with my life right now
I curl up and sleep

In life, a monster,
a racist, and closet drunk.
In death, an angel.

A million others
Talk and think the way we do
We're not so unique

Outlawed immigrants
Good enough for housekeeping
But not for neighbors

My pen is my voice
Telling the world of my thoughts
Please don't mistake them

So desperate for love
I risk driving you away
I can't help myself

Just arrived at work
Yet already counting down
Until you can leave

Can't argue with them
They always think they are right
My stubborn parents

Death is not the worst
We always think it is so
Life can be much worse

Look at you and think
One day you'll no longer be
I can't stand that day

Toilet seat left up
No gift on Valentine's Day
No wonder wives nag

The best she knew how
That was the way she loved me
Less than I deserved

Shaky foundations
Relationships built on lies
Will always collapse

Cheesy pick up lines
For the most desperate men
It's their last resort

The other woman
Never thought she'd be the one
To play homewrecker

Do I want children?
Answer yes as a woman
And risk your career

Our stereotypes
If they were not sometimes true
They would not exist

For divorced parents
Children can become weapons
In their civil war

Innocent women
Taken and raped by soldiers
War breeds callousness

Liquor ad's sweet lie
Drink their product and become
Catnip to women

Bread winning father
Gets the job of being Dad
Without all the stress

Story of a girl
She captured my heart one day
Set it free the next

Jealousy ensures
Women will always have to
Deal with cattiness

Eating at midnight
Stuffing her face with desserts
Still can't fill the void

World's hardest metal
Wasted on fine jewelry
Because it sparkles

Many men's folly
Falling in love with women
For whom they must pay

American dream
Get rich quickly with the least
Amount of effort

                    Sins of the parents
              They do visit the offspring
                  And never leave them

Cures all of your ills
Tears stand no chance against them
Hugs from a mother

              The most worthless word
          Used when more helpful ones can't
                be thought of: sorry.

Lie told to children
Doing good leads to good things
Being done to you

The price of duty
Doing what you don't want to
For the sake of others

The prison system
Meant from criminal rehab
Used for networking

All you need is love
Until the mortgage is due
Then you need money

My life before you
I thought that I was living
Now I know better

So afraid of math
People prefer being wrong
To accuracy

Just one of many
No matter your "uniqueness"
Thousands are like you

Try being honest
Then count your number of friends
Lying has value

People flock outside
To act like wild animals
I hate nice weather

Battle for loudness
To cancel out your noise, I make
more. No one wins.

Waiting for the day
When you realize the sad truth
I don't deserve you

We all seek the same:
To escape reality.
Drugs are but one way

How many scandals
Before we realize famous
People aren't perfect

Bearer of bad news
Most children are average
It had to be said

Silly denial
To say you were not asleep
When you really were

Complete paradox
So much ignorance in the
Information Age

The best of my friends
Used to call him Worm, now it's
John Brickhouse, Esquire

Sparkling white today
Then filthy again next week
Cleaning is a waste

Same as your muscles
Your brain needs some exercise
Else it turns to mush

Constant horn blaring
The traffic ignores it all
Pointless noise making

For far too many
Loudness is a way of life
Quiet down, people

See funny movie
Then quote it for the next month
Life imitates art

Oh man, that's my jam
All the verses I ignore
The hook all I know

No more hateful group
Than religious extremists
Christian or Muslim

Why bother learning
About different cultures?
Hate is easier

Stuck on endless loop
Wake up, work, then back to bed
My life on repeat

Happiness for sale
Anytime money wants it
It can be purchased

The girl mattered not
All I cared about was love
Little did she now

All I've ever felt
Has been written down in song
How I love music

Three wishes I got
All I needed was the one
For you to love me

To excuse cheating
I focus on my wife's faults
When she is flawless

Give me back my heart
You were too careless with it
Now it is broken

Finite resources
For an overcrowded world
Something has to give

When I am with you
I forget what sadness is
You are my Prozac

I am not perfect
But for you I will try to
Be with all my might

Sometimes words fail me
All I'll say is I love you
And hope that's enough

My heart you did touch
With the most thoughtful gesture
I've ever received

Why must happiness
The most pleasant emotion
Be all too fleeting

Irony's meaning
We think we know what it is
But most of us don't

Used to be our song
But now that we've broken up
I cannot stand it

What a waste of time
All the weeks and months I spent
Falling for your lies

What Facebook taught us
That we are all narcissists
With the right outlet

Bundled up warmly
Stranger asks if I am cold
I just roll my eyes

Throughout history
What have humans been best at?
Killing each other.

When it is us, it
is legal. When it is them,
it's terrorism.

Large pile of litter
Lies inches from a trash can
Unbelievable

Women have men fooled
They claim they're worth the effort
But are they really

Forbidden kisses
Stolen behind the school house
Always taste so sweet

An overused word
Perhaps once it had meaning
What is love, Alex?

Under construction
That's what my heart is now that
You have shattered it

After you left me
First I felt extreme sadness
Then I felt relief

It won't be okay
Please refrain from saying that
I know lies from truth

At our first hello
Our time started running out
Love has an end date

Our real, flawed romance
Nothing in some fairy tale
Could top what we have

Take this sadness gun
So even when I'm not here
You remain happy